HOSPITAL

That's Gross!
A Look at Science

Julie Murray

Big Buddy BOOKS
That's Gross!

VISIT US AT
www.abdopublishing.com

Published by ABDO Publishing Company, 8000 West 78th Street, Edina, Minnesota 55439.

Printed in the United States.

Coordinating Series Editor: Rochelle Baltzer
Editor: Sarah Tieck
Contributing Editor: Marcia Zappa
Graphic Design: Deborah Coldiron
Cover Photographs: *iStockPhoto:* Bojan Fatur, iStockPhoto, Michal Rozanski.
Interior Photographs/Illustrations: *iStockPhoto:* Monika Adamczyk (p. 29), Jani Bryson (pp. 10, 14, 27), David Hernandez (p. 30), Lisa Howard (p. 7), iStockPhoto (pp. 6, 27, 29), Bonnie Jacobs (p. 12), Bela Tibor Kozma (p. 20), Cat London (p. 28), Carmen Martinez (p. 29), Steve Shepard (p. 21), Mike Sonnenberg (p. 8, 16, 22); *Photo Researchers, Inc.:* Mike Devlin (p. 13), Pascal Goetgheluck (p. 17), Louis Murray (p. 23, 30), St. Bartholomew's Hospital (p. 19); *Photos.com:* Jupiter Images (pp. 5, 9, 11, 15, 25).

Library of Congress Cataloging-in-Publication Data

Murray, Julie, 1969-
 Hospital / Julie Murray.
   p. cm. -- (That's gross! A look at science)
 ISBN 978-1-60453-556-3
 1. Hospitals--Juvenile literature. 2. Hospital care--Juvenile literature. I. Title.
 RA963.5.M87 2009
 363.11--dc22
                          2008036381

Contents

Exploring the Hospital

The hospital is amazing! Doctors help. **Patients** (PAY-shuhnts) heal. And, lives are saved. Look a little closer. You'll see that behind all that cool stuff is a lot of yuck. Some of it is natural. Some of it is unhealthy. Let's explore!

Wash Your Hands!

Have you ever noticed how often doctors wash their hands? Today, doctors and nurses know it is important to be clean. But, things weren't always that way.

More than 100 years ago, most doctors did not wash their hands. Their fingers were caked in dirt, blood, and body **fluids** (FLOO-uhds). Doctors unknowingly helped spread sicknesses!

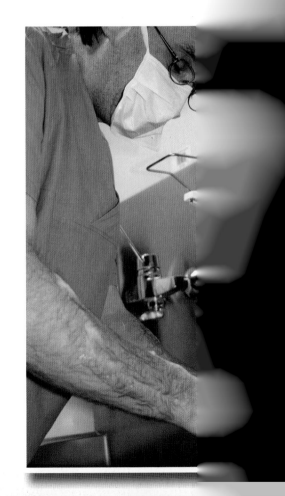

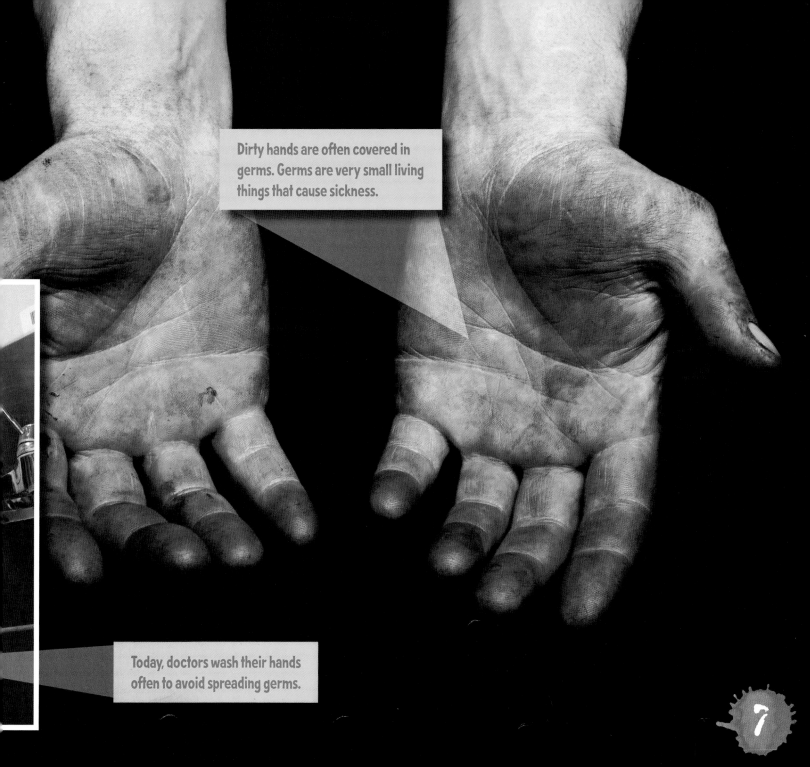

Dirty hands are often covered in germs. Germs are very small living things that cause sickness.

Today, doctors wash their hands often to avoid spreading germs.

7

Dirty History

Hospitals used to be dirty places. Hospital workers didn't know about **germs** (JUHRMS) and how important it was not to spread them. So, they didn't always clean up blood or wash **medical** tools.

Nurses were often untrained. They would put more than one **patient** in a bed. Sometimes, a healing patient shared a bed with someone who was dead or dying!

In the 1800s, famous nurse Florence Nightingale helped clean up hospitals.

9

Today, most hospitals are very neat. Doctors and nurses go to school for many years. And, they know how important it is to keep things clean.

But, gross things still happen at hospitals. For example, people get sick and throw up. And, doctors have to touch blood and gooey body parts. This can't be helped. It is just ordinary at a hospital! But today, workers clean up after touching these gross things.

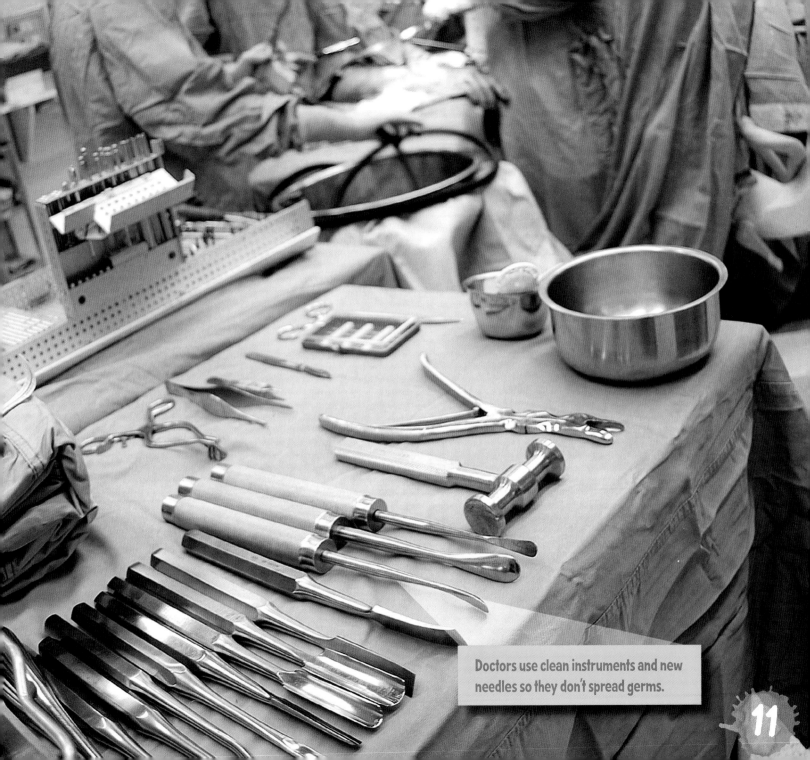

Doctors use clean instruments and new needles so they don't spread germs.

Stuck in Bed

For some people in the hospital, it is hard to get up and move. Some **patients** are too sick to get out of bed.

These patients may get **sores** on their skin from not moving. These are called bedsores. Bedsores form because body parts aren't getting enough blood flow. This causes the skin to get sick.

People often get bedsores on their heels. Other common places include the back, elbows, and hips. People can get very sick or even die from infected bedsores.

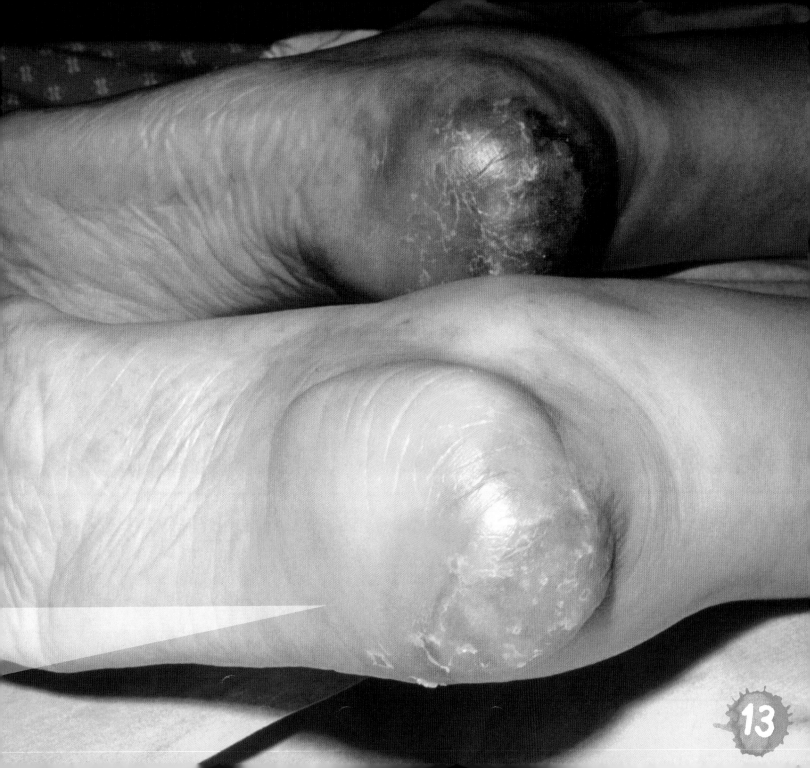

Patients that are stuck in bed still need to poop and pee! So, hospitals have special bowls that people can use as toilets in bed. These are called bedpans. Bedpans don't flush. So once they're full, someone has to empty them. Yuck!

Bedpans can be metal or plastic. Some get thrown away after they are used. Others can be reused.

That's just gross!

Sometimes, sick people get constipated. This makes it hard to poop. So, doctors shoot air or liquid into their intestines to help clean them out. This is called an enema.

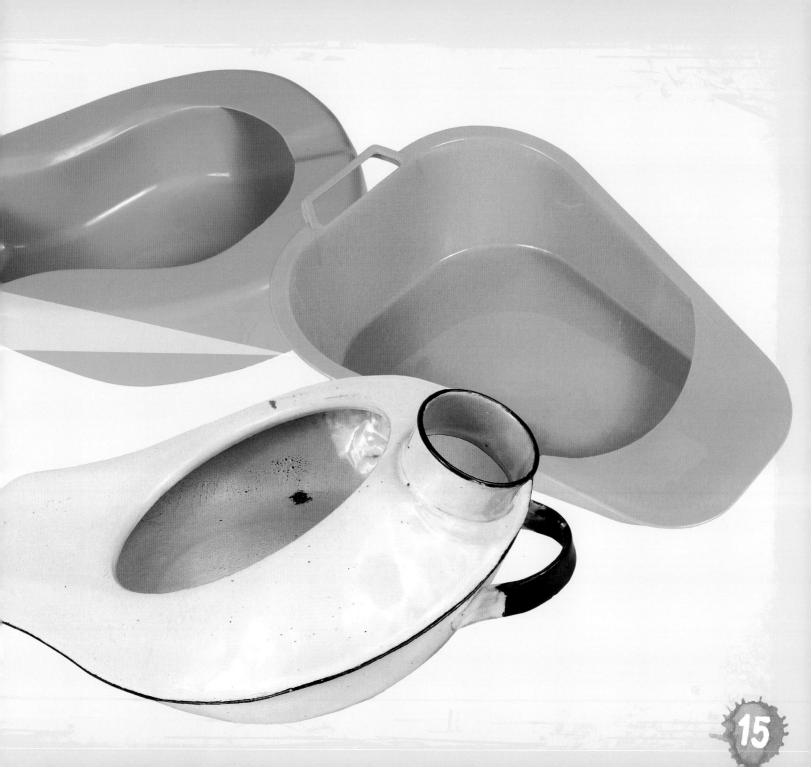

Bloodsuckers

If you went swimming and found a leech on your toe, you'd probably scream. But sometimes at hospitals, leeches are put on people's skin on purpose! They suck blood to help people heal.

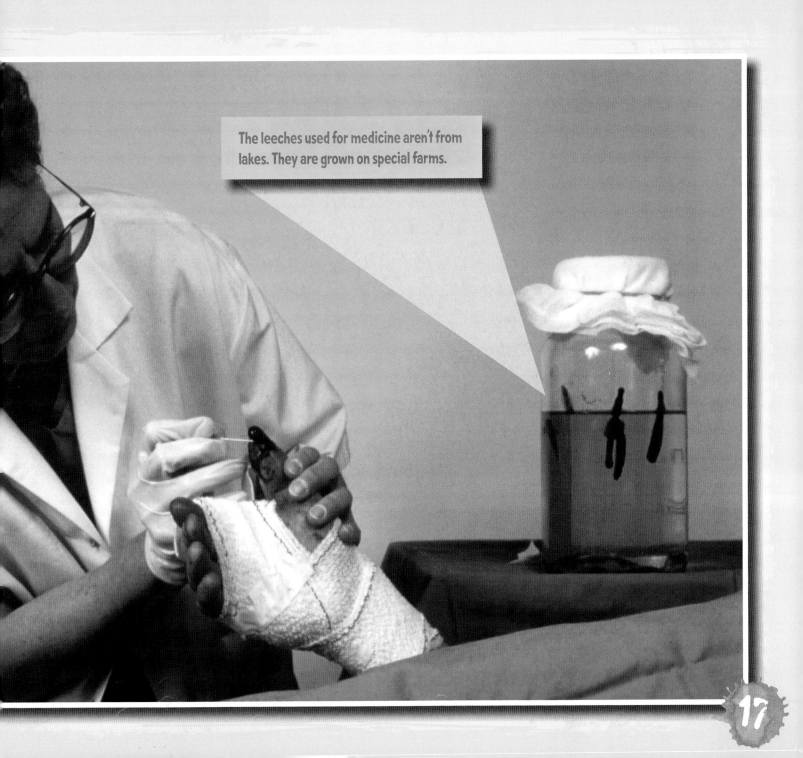

17

The idea of using leeches is not new. Doctors have used leeches for thousands of years! Long ago, people believed it was healthy to let leeches suck their blood. Today, doctors know that this helps with some problems, but not all sicknesses.

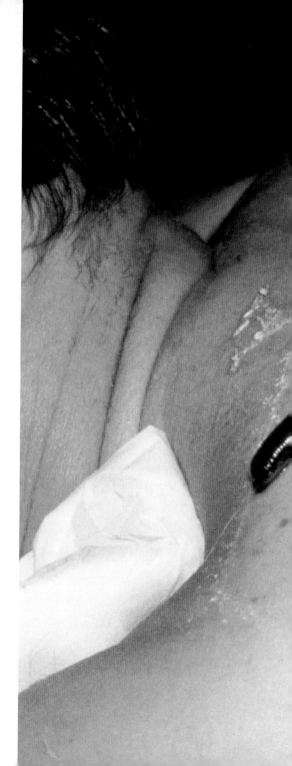

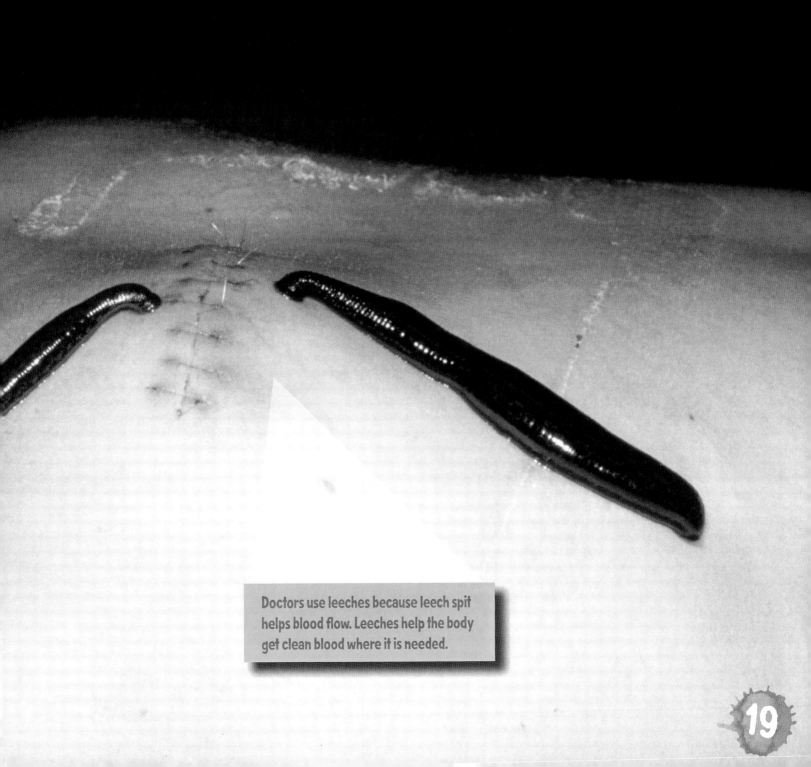

Doctors use leeches because leech spit helps blood flow. Leeches help the body get clean blood where it is needed.

Burning up
Hospitals used to burn medical waste. Today, medical waste has to be cleaned before it can be burned or thrown away.

What's in the Garbage?

Sometimes, doctors use disposable tools, such as needles. They also use bandages and rags. And, they may cut out tumors (TOO-muhrs) or body parts.

All of these items must be thrown away. But, they are often covered with blood and other goo. Body fluids can spread sicknesses. So, medical waste is thrown away in special containers (kuhn-TAY-nuhrs). When people touch medical waste, they wear gloves to guard their hands.

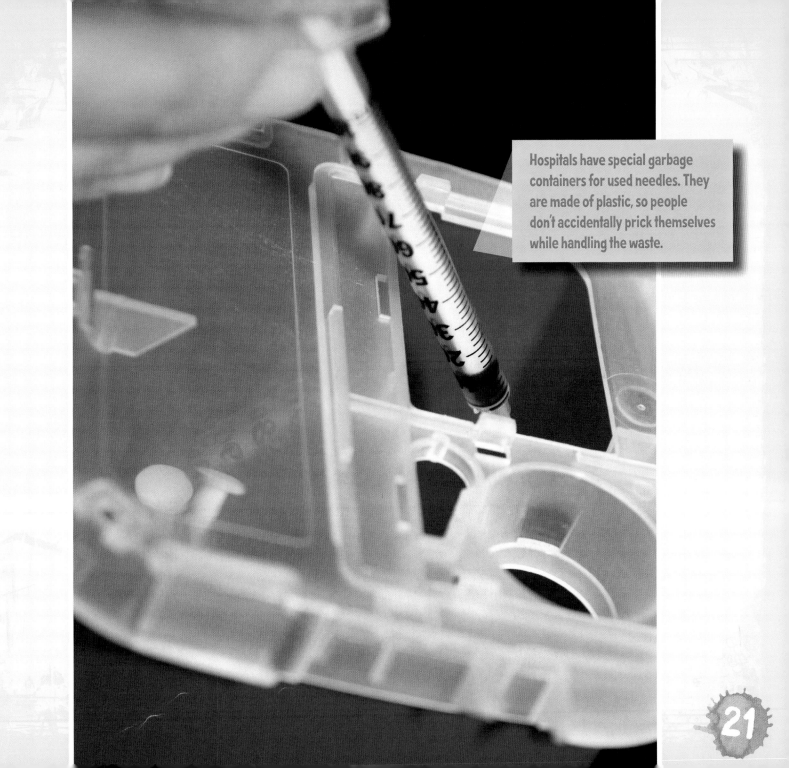

Hospitals have special garbage containers for used needles. They are made of plastic, so people don't accidentally prick themselves while handling the waste.

Pus for Dinner

Can you imagine your doctor putting bugs into a big cut? Sometimes wounds become infected and filled with yellowish goo called pus (PUHS). It is very hard for an infected wound to heal. Sometimes it can't.

One way to fight infection is to place baby flies called maggots into open wounds. Maggots eat dead tissue (TIH-shoo). Though the use of maggots is uncommon, this has saved some lives!

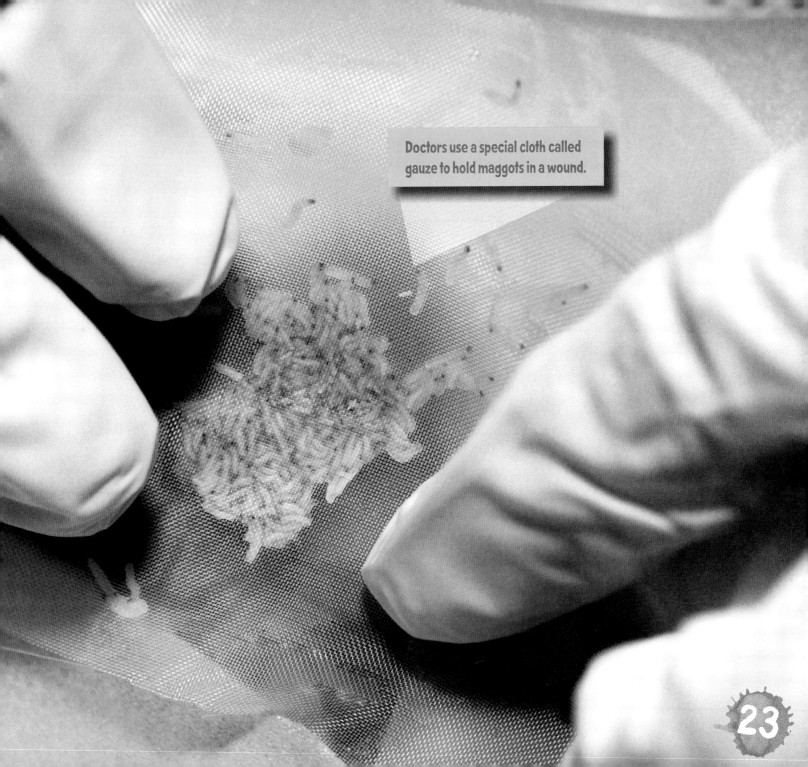

Doctors use a special cloth called gauze to hold maggots in a wound.

Shot-stravaganza

Shots are nothing to fear! It's important to get your immunization (ih-myuh-nuh-ZAY-shuhn) shots. Yes, they kind of hurt. And, it is even more gross if you know what is in that little tube.

Very small amounts of certain **germs** are in shots. But, these germs don't make people sick. In fact, putting a small amount of germs in someone's body can make it stronger. This can help the person fight off larger germs.

24

Shots that prevent sicknesses are called immunization shots. They have helped many people stay healthy.

25

Stitch It Up

When someone has a very deep cut or **surgery** (SUHRJ-ree), stitches might be necessary. Doctors sew the skin together using a thread and needle. This helps close the skin so the body can heal it.

When healing is done, some stitches **dissolve** or come out on their own. Other times, doctors must cut them and pull them out! Snip, snip, snip.

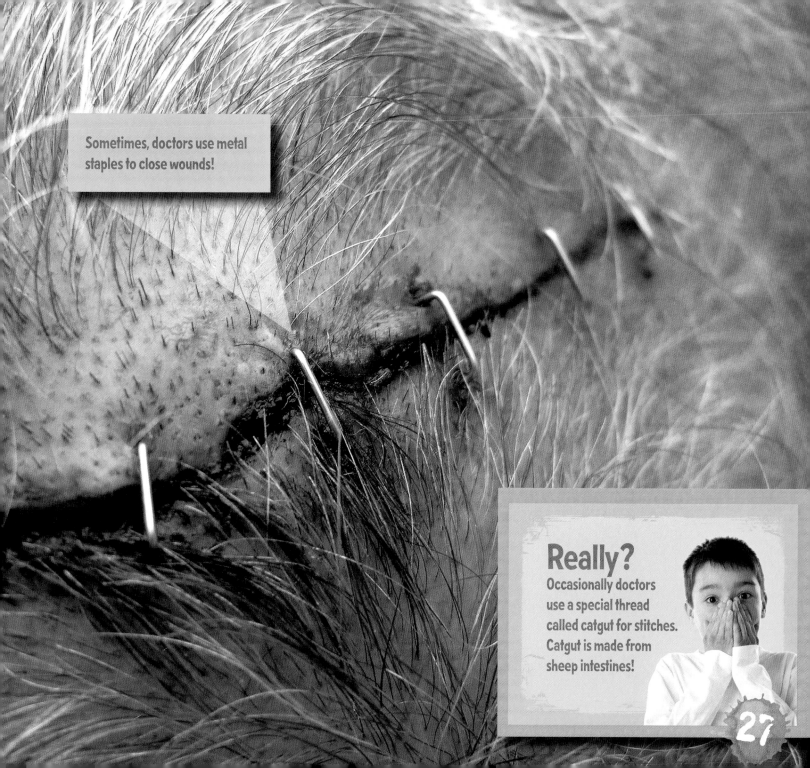

Sometimes, doctors use metal staples to close wounds!

Really?
Occasionally doctors use a special thread called catgut for stitches. Catgut is made from sheep intestines!

27

That WAS Gross!

Between **germ**-filled shots, dirty bedpans, and oozing blood, some pretty yucky things are at hospitals.

Now that you know about all the grossness, take a closer look! Many gross things are just a part of life and no big deal. Others can be prevented. Do what you can to live in a healthy way!

Washing your hands helps keep germs out of your body. This prevents sickness.

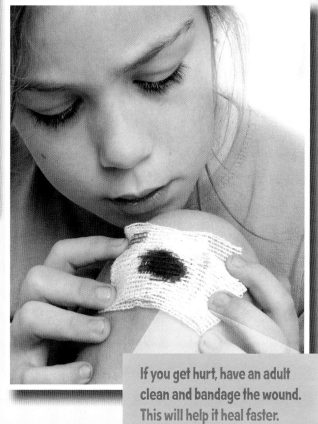

If you get hurt, have an adult clean and bandage the wound. This will help it heal faster.

You can't escape germs. They're everywhere! But eating healthy and getting enough rest helps your body fight them off.

Eeeeww! What is THAT?

Answer on page 32.

Answer on page 32.

30

Important Words

container a box, bottle, or something else used to hold something.

disposable meant to be thrown away after use.

dissolve to separate into small bits.

fluid a liquid.

flush to wash out with a sudden flow of water.

germs harmful organisms that can make people sick.

infected made sick by something harmful entering the body.

medical of or relating to medicine. Medicine is the science that deals with health and sickness prevention.

patient a person who is under the care of a doctor.

sore a painful place on the body where the skin is infected, broken, or bruised.

surgery the treating of sickness or injury by cutting into and repairing body parts.

tissue a group of similar cells working together.

tumor an abnormal clump of cells.

Web Sites

To learn more about gross stuff, visit ABDO Publishing Company online. Web sites about gross stuff are featured on our Book Links page. These links are routinely monitored and updated to provide the most current information available.

www.abdopublishing.com

Index

"Eeeeww! What Is THAT?" answer: maggots in a wound.